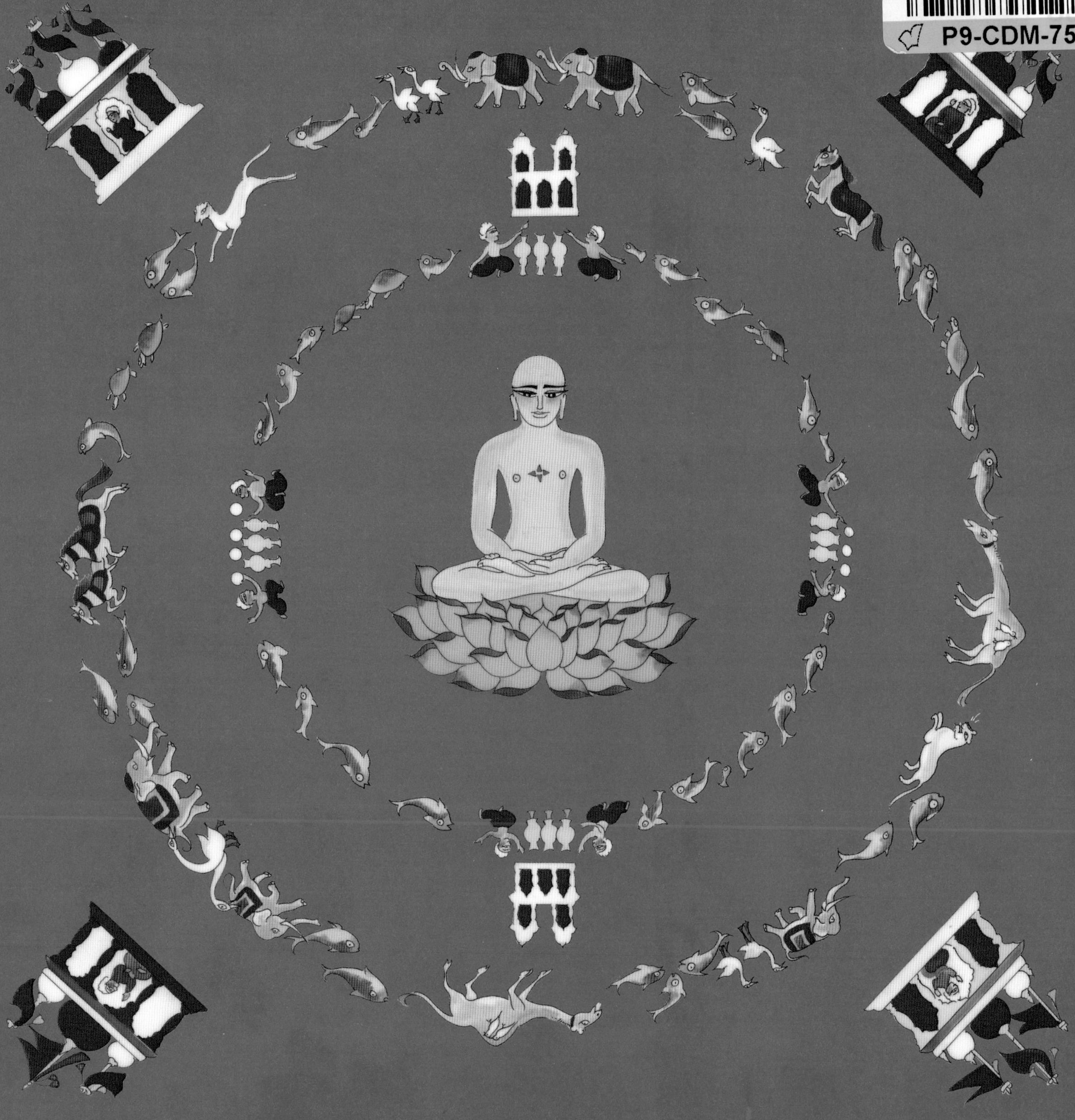

To my parents, Vinay and Laxmi and my in-laws Kushal and Maan
whose devotion to the Jain way of life is my inspiration.   —M.J.

Dedicated to Peace, "Far better than a thousand words is
one word that brings peace." -Dhammapada   —Demi

Mahavira: The Hero of Nonviolence © Manoj Jain and Demi 2014
Wisdom Tales is an imprint of World Wisdom, Inc.
All rights reserved.
No part of this book may be used or reproduced in any manner
without written permission, except in critical articles and reviews.
The illustrations are rendered in mixed media.
Book Design by Michael Nelson

Printed in China on acid-free paper
Production Date: January 2014
Plant & Location: Printed by 1010 Printing International Ltd
Job / Batch #: TT13080405
For information address Wisdom Tales,
P. O. Box 2682, Bloomington, Indiana 47402-2682
www. wisdomtalespress.com

LIBRARY OF CONGRESS CATALOGING-IN-PUBLICATION DATA
Jain, Manoj, author.
Mahavira : the hero of nonviolence / By Manoj Jain ; Illustrated by Demi.
pages cm
ISBN 978-1-937786-21-2 (hardcover : alk. paper)
1. Mahavira—Juvenile literature. 2. Tirthankaras—Biography—Juvenile literature.
I. Demi, illustrator. II. Title.
BL1371.J328 2014   294.4092—dc23   [B]   2013050111

MAHAVIRA AND JAINISM

Mahavira is the twenty-fourth spiritual teacher of the Jain religion, which has its original roots in India. A contemporary of Gautama Buddha, Mahavira propagated the universal ethic of nonviolence in the sixth century BCE. Renouncing the world at the age of thirty, he devoted twelve years to deep meditation, after which he attained enlightenment. For the next thirty years he traveled from village to village teaching nonviolence towards all living beings.

In addition to nonviolence, the central theme of Jainism is non-absolutism, which means that we must realize that real truth has multiple facets, and non-possessiveness, which means that we must balance our needs with our desires. These three core practices help us manage our anger, ego, deceit, and greed.

Today there are ten million followers of Jainism worldwide. With its emphasis on the sanctity of all life, Jains live a life of compassion and forgiveness and promote a vegetarian diet and ecological practices. Jainism has influenced many, including Mahatma Gandhi, the most revered nonviolent leader in the world.

Live and Help Live
JAINA

The author, illustrator, and publisher would like to extend their appreciation to JAINA (The Federation of Jain Associations in North America) for their support and assistance in making this book possible. JAINA represents eighty Jain temples and centers and 120,000 Jains in North America with the goal of sharing the Jain teaching and way of life.

JAINA gratefully acknowledges the contributions by: Prem and Sandhya Jain (CA), Suman and Sital Jain (NY), Kamlesh and Leena Parekh (MS), Ajit Jain (CT), Sushil and Preeti Jain (IN), Mukesh and Neelam Jain (TN), Amit and Rachana Jain (CA), Yogendra and Preeti Jain (MA), Sunit and Seema Jain (IL), Vinay and Laxmi Jain (MA), Kushal and Maan Jain (IL), Bhagwan Mahavir Endowed Professorship of Jain Studies at the Florida International University, Jain Education and Research Foundation (FL).

MAHAVIRA
THE HERO OF NONVIOLENCE

BY MANOJ JAIN   ILLUSTRATED BY DEMI

Wisdom Tales

THE BIRTH
OF MAHAVIRA

IN A FARAWAY LAND
called India, a great leader was
born on this earth. He came to
teach people how to live a life
free of violence.

His story began in a high mountain kingdom more than 2,600 years ago. One night Queen Trishala had a dream. In her dream she saw many fine objects. There was a lion, an elephant, a pair of fish. There was also a garland, a flag, and smokeless fire.

The next morning the queen described the sacred dream to her husband, King Siddhartha. The king gathered his astrologers. They were to interpret the meaning of this dream.

The astrologers soon agreed. "The queen will give birth to a special child. He will show the spiritual path of nonviolence to the world."

The king and queen were filled with happiness.

During the queen's pregnancy much changed. The rains arrived seasonally. The crops grew plentifully. And the people laughed happily. The astrologers said that these were the blessing of the child to come.

Some months later the great moment arrived. On a clear moonlit night, at midnight, a boy was born to the queen. The whole kingdom was overjoyed!

Soon it came time to name the young prince. The king said, "Our land has enjoyed great happiness and good fortune since the prince's birth. So we will call him Vardhaman, which means 'ever-increasing.'"

THE YOUNG PRINCE

Young Vardhaman quickly learned the sixty-four arts and sciences. He was skilled in math, reading, horse riding, astronomy, and many other subjects. But what interested him most was the meaning of life. He wanted a path for his soul to follow.

As a young prince, he practiced the Jain way of life. Jains believe in nonviolence. They have deep respect and compassion for all living beings, including animals and plants. So great is their love for animals that they do not eat meat. They are vegetarians.

One day, the prince was playing with his friends in the forest. He challenged them. "The first one to climb the tree will be the winner!"

As he raced up the tree, he saw his friends run away in fear. The prince turned around. Suddenly he saw a fearsome snake ready to bite him!

Without fear the prince picked up the snake. He had the strength to crush it with his bare hands. But the prince did not wish to kill another living being. He had respect for all forms of life. And so he chose to lead the snake away to a safe place.

His friends watched in awe. News of the prince's bravery and compassion spread to the city. Soon the people began calling him Mahavira, which means "very brave."

Living in the Palace

Mahavira lived as a prince in the palace. But he longed for something more. He searched for the truth and for knowledge of the soul.

Then, when he was just twenty-eight years old, Mahavira's parents died. He saw that all life is temporary and must end. He saw that life goes through times of happiness and times of sadness.

Mahavira wanted to begin a spiritual journey to find the meaning of life. And so he asked the blessing of his older brother to become a monk, a holy man.

Mahavira's brother was kind and generous. But he asked that Mahavira wait for two years before leaving. Obeying his brother's wishes, Mahavira agreed. During this time the prince grew more and more generous. Each day he donated thousands of gold coins to those in need.

THE SPIRITUAL JOURNEY

Mahavira's brother could
see the young prince's strong
dedication to the spiritual
life. And so he gave Mahavira
permission to leave the worldly
life. The prince became a monk!

A long line of people
escorted Mahavira to the
forest. There he gave up his
princely jewels and clothing.
He said farewell to his family
and his kingdom.

Then Mahavira started on
the spiritual journey. With great
focus and devotion he achieved
the three spiritual "jewels."
In Jainism these are called
right faith, right knowledge,
and right conduct.

The first jewel is right faith. It is to believe that the clean and pure soul is divine in nature.

———❖———

The second jewel is right knowledge. It is to see the difference between the living and the non-living. Humans, animals, and plants are all living. They have a soul. Houses, tables, and computers are non-living. They don't have a soul.

———❖———

The third jewel is right conduct. It means to put right faith and right knowledge into practice. Right conduct means not to hurt other living things. It means not to think, say, or do anything harmful.

IN THE FOREST

For twelve long years Mahavira
traveled in the forest. There
he spent his time in deep
meditation. Day by day his
soul became purer and purer.

Mahavira's meditation had
many steps. First, he relaxed his
body by sitting still. Then, he
calmed his mind by taking deep
breaths. Last, he cleared his
mind of all thoughts. Thus he
gained knowledge of the soul.

One day Mahavira was
walking on the banks
of a river. As he began
to meditate, he heard a
voice warning him. "This
place is haunted! Terrible
demons will not let you
stay here!"

But Mahavira
thought to himself,
"I love all creatures.
I fear no-one and no-
one fears me. And so I
will meditate here unharmed."

As the night came, a mighty
demon appeared. It raced
towards Mahavira in the form
of a mad elephant. With its
sharp tusks it picked him up
and threw him into the air.
But Mahavira's great power
of peace kept him unhurt
and unafraid.

The mighty demon saw that Mahavira was filled with love and compassion. He said, "In my anger I have wrongly tried to kill you. Now I see that you are a great and powerful soul. Please forgive me."

Mahavira replied calmly: "Anger has led you to cruelty and revenge. It can only be defeated by forgiveness and love. Only they can end the violence. Only they can bring you peace."

The story of Mahavira and the demon is a reminder of how we must all forgive. Just as in North America there is a day for giving thanks, Thanksgiving Day, so Jains have a day for asking forgiveness, Forgiveness Day. On this day, families and friends meet each other. They call each other. They write to each other. They ask forgiveness for whatever they have said or done to hurt others.

TEACHING OF WISDOM

At the age of forty-two, Mahavira reached the goal of the spiritual path. His soul had become completely pure. He had full knowledge of all things in the past, present, and future.

For the next thirty years
Mahavira taught others about
the spiritual life. He showed
them how to reach the truth,
and how to become free of
suffering. He instructed them
on the three main beliefs
of Jainism.

The first belief is nonviolence or love. It is not to cause harm to any living being. It is to have love and compassion for all living things. To do this, a person must avoid anger and learn to forgive.

———— ⚬⚬⚬ ————

The second belief is non-absolutism or pluralism. It is to tolerate and accept another person's view, to keep an open mind. And if there are disagreements, to understand that the truth has many sides. To do this, a person must avoid pride and learn to be humble.

———— ⚬⚬⚬ ————

The third belief is non-possessiveness or detachment. It is to separate true needs from false desires. To do this, a person must avoid greed and learn to be charitable.

Mahavira lived and traveled in Northern India. During this time, there lived another great teacher, the Buddha. Although the two never met, both taught the truth about the spiritual life. The religion of the Buddha, Buddhism, spread from India to East Asia. The religion of Mahavira, Jainism, remained in India. But today both religions have expanded throughout the world.

The teachings of Mahavira were very popular. All living beings, including animals, would gather to listen to his words of peace. Each would understand Mahavira in their own language. The lion would sit down with the lamb, and the king with the beggar. Each would respect the other. For they could see a living soul, and not just a body, in their neighbor.

At the age of seventy-two, after giving his last sermon, Mahavira left this world. His soul reached *moksha*. In *moksha* there is no pain, suffering, or sadness. It is a place of knowledge, happiness, and bliss.

On this day, all living things rejoiced. They knew that Mahavira's soul had been freed from this world. Since then, the Jains celebrate the festival of Diwali on this day. They eat tasty sweets and sing religious songs. And they visit family and friends and exchange gifts.

JAINISM TODAY

The message of Mahavira
has lasted for thousands of
years. To this day it influences
millions of people. Mahatma
Gandhi, India's spiritual
leader, learned his practice
of nonviolence from a Jain
teacher. His mother was greatly
influenced by Jain monks.
Gandhi spent many hours
learning how nonviolence
could be used in dealing with
society's problems. He used
it to fight for India's freedom
from British rule.

Others learned from Gandhi. In the United States, Martin Luther King, Jr. used nonviolence to bring equal rights for African-Americans.

Imagine bringing justice, equality, and peace to the world. And imagine doing so without using violence. Such is the teaching of Mahavira and of Jainism.

Who will be the next person to take this message of nonviolence and make our world a better place? Perhaps you?